OUR FATHER

OUR FATHER

Ron Pinkston

Pleasant Word
A Division of WINEPRESS PUBLISHING

Printed in the United States of America

Packaged by Pleasant Word, a division of WinePress Publishing, PO Box 428, Enumclaw, WA 98022. The views expressed or implied in this work do not necessarily reflect those of Pleasant Word, a division of WinePress Publishing. Ultimate design, content, and editorial accuracy of this work are the responsibilities of the author.

ISBN 1-4141-0065-5
Library of Congress Catalog Card Number: 2003114001

Dedication

With all the love in my heart, I dedicate this book to my beloved wife, Susan. For over 31 years she has stood by me and made me a better man through Christ's love.

Table of Contents

Acknowledgements

First of all, I would like to express my deepest appreciation to Dr. Dan Fox, M.D., whose vision and passion made this book possible. It was his determined posture and tireless personal effort, overriding my objections, that took these teachings from the auditorium to the reading audience.

Secondly, I want to thank Lisa Shera for her incredible patience and assistance in coordinating the team of people who proofread and edited the manuscript. And to those many readers and editors, my heartfelt thanks go out to you for all the hard work.

Finally, I owe a huge debt of gratitude to the East Bay Fellowship Staff and congregation. Without their partnership I would have little to say and no platform from which to speak. I am humbled and honored to be your pastor and friend in Jesus.

Endorsements

"Clear . . . concise . . . practical" are the marks of effective pastoral communication. In *Our Father*, Ron Pinkston combines his God-given gifts and skills as an outstanding pastor, denominational leader, and mentor of others to bring us a hands-on understanding of the model for our praying. It is *clear* in the use of modern-day terminology and illustrations; it is *concise* in getting to the point of what Jesus wanted to convey; and it is *practical* in offering concrete steps in making the

Lord's Prayer *yours*. It is a must for your reading enjoyment and benefit.

—Paul Risser

President, International

Church of the Foursquare Gospel

The word *prayer* can strike fear in the heart, and another book on prayer can be terrifying! The reason is simple: I don't pray very well or nearly enough. But when Ron pulled up a chair and sat down with my heart and I heard the practical words of one of my dearest friends, I found myself captivated again by the magnificence and beauty of our Lord's Prayer. This is no guilt trip, but rather a simple and gracious invitation to keep learning from the heart of Jesus to pray—not in sterile towers of religious ritual, but in the everyday dustiness of my life.

This little book will be a welcome friend on my spiritual trek.

—Jerry Cook

Foreword

Most of us who sincerely want to follow Jesus' instructions and counsel for life get stuck, periodically, on truths we can't quite grasp with natural thought processes (forgiving grievances, turning the other cheek, scattering our wealth generously, etc.). In addition to those kinds of mind-bogglers, there are several patterns of profound spiritual life that can seem unattainable to normal, *barely-able-to-keep-our-chins-above-the-water-as-we-doggie-paddle* believers. Prayer is one such biggie.

On the one hand, we feel guilty for not praying *more;* on the other, we often feel too rotten about ourselves and what we've (just) done to pray at all. Even though it is the furthest thing from God's heart, we get stymied by always coming up short in a personal assessment of how *much* we pray.

As if that weren't enough of a heavy load to try dragging along in our spiritual walk, we also find ourselves facing huge questions about how *well* we pray. Did we say it right? Is there a proper order to our requests? Is there a correct salutation and closing? That's why many people feel so uncomfortable praying aloud with others.

In this encouraging, delightful, and very practical book, Ron Pinkston offers us an antidote to these common struggles with prayer that plague most Christians. You'll quickly see that prayer isn't just a morning exercise, a set verbal exchange with God, but an entire atmosphere for life. By parsing through the Lord's Prayer (the words Jesus used to teach His friends the very things we want to know about how to pray better), Ron offers us simple, yet rich insights that will change people's ideas about talking to God.

I'm not at all surprised to see such a gentle, kind, yet straightforward book come from Ron's heart, for in our friendship of nearly 30 years, I have observed, time and time again, a man whose constant thoughts are of others—how to help and love and encourage. The way he loves his wife, Sue; the way he tirelessly serves his hugely successful congregation; the manner in which he always seems to ask people about the littlest details that make such a big statement about how he cares—all these give evidence of a man whose life has been utterly transformed by God.

The Bible says of Jesus that He taught as one having *authority* (insight, expertise), not like the scribes who merely parroted religious words. When He spoke, people like you and me felt understood and encouraged, and what He shared gave insight into wonderful mysteries. So it is with sheer pleasure that I recommend this book on prayer written by a true authority.

—Daniel A. Brown, Ph.D.
Aptos, 2003

Preface

I wrote this book because I know the feelings of helplessness and powerlessness that we've all felt at some time in life, the same feelings that many are experiencing in this postmodern era. Everywhere it seems people are searching for personal fulfillment in an attempt to give meaning to their lives, as if they could do nothing to actually *change* their lives. But there is something that can (and will) radically change your life. It is not a new exercise program, career plan, or romance. You can't purchase it at any price (the price has already been paid for you!). It's called *prayer.* Almost everyone believes in prayer. But not everyone understands it. This book is an attempt to help us all understand a little better the power there is in prayer.

Prayer changed my life!

Thirty-plus years ago I asked God to show me He was real, and He turned the next 30 days of my life upside down. I was drafted into the Army, filled with the Holy Spirit (I didn't even know there was a Holy Spirit when I prayed that prayer), and stationed in Germany within those 30 days. By the end of that time I had no choice but to believe.

Around the same time I asked God to help me give up the love I had for my girlfriend (who was no longer interested in me—in fact, hated me and swore she would never marry me), and a week later she proposed marriage to me. We've been married for 31 years as of this writing.

One day years later, my life was buried in unforgiveness and I asked God to help me. He did a miracle in my heart and showed me that no one owes me anything, a principle that continues to set me free from the offenses of others.

Another time a man committed himself to destroy my leadership by talking to those who worked with me and telling them what a bad person I was. I asked God what to do, and He said, "Nothing. Leave it to Me." That was so hard, but I obeyed, and to my complete amazement not one of those people the man talked to took his side. They all came to me and revealed what was happening. Together we prayed, and that man (who was probably the most prominent leader in our congregation at the time) left without even creating a ripple. It was amazing.

Last year the radio program I am privileged to do was coming up for renewal, and I felt it was necessary for me to offer to our Church Council to take the program off the air so that we could use those finances for other things. Then I asked God if He wanted it on the air. If so, I needed Him to show me so I could respond with integrity. The next week a man invited me to lunch and asked (with no knowledge of my prayer or our Church Council's commitment) in essence if he could pay for the radio program for an entire year.

Last week . . . well, you get the idea. Those are just some highlights of a life dependent on prayer. I admit I have nothing to offer without God. But with Him there are no impossibilities. And no one knows better than I how un-special I am. I'm just a regular guy who loves Jesus. If these things (and a thousand more) can happen for me, what can happen for you?

Please read this book and discover the answer to that question for yourself. I will not receive a penny from this book. I just want to share with anyone who will listen the secret to a life of power with God. I hope you'll read and pray. I'll be praying for you.

An Awesome Life

Are you happy with your life? Is it everything you hoped it would be? Have you ever thought there must be something better or more fulfilling? Do the daily routines of life seem to drain all the passion from you? Here's the good news. Each day holds more possibilities than you or I can fathom. And God wants you to have more than just an ordinary life; He wants you to have an awesome life that is interesting and full of hope, love, and joy on a daily basis.

In the movie *Meet the Parents*, Ben Stiller portrays a young man who is called upon to pray over a meal with his fiancée's family and completely bungles the job. His intentions are great but he obviously has never prayed before. It's a pathetically painful scene filled with awkward moments. It would have been better if he'd just said, "Sir, I don't know how to pray." But apparently that would have been too embarrassing. So he launched into the unknown and created a much greater and longer moment of embarrassment.

In some ways that scene reminds me of what it's like when people try to pray in the real world. When you ask people on the street if they pray, you'll almost always get a positive response. But if you ask someone to pray on the spot, things get real tense fairly quickly. Wouldn't it be great if we really knew what we were doing in prayer? Wouldn't you love to have someone ask you to pray and suddenly feel a surge of electricity go through your body, telling you that you're up to it? More importantly, wouldn't you love to be able to talk to God in a way that works . . . every day?

Well, that's what this book is about. It's really simple. In Matthew 6, verses 9–13, Jesus taught His disciples how to pray, and ultimately their prayers (and the resulting actions) changed the whole world, even our calendars.

Here's the good news right up front: The disciples were lousy at praying when they started out. In fact, there's no real record of them praying at all during the three years they followed Jesus while He walked with them on earth. He's caught praying frequently, at virtually any time of the day or night. But they don't pray. It isn't until they do pray (after He returns to heaven) that things really start to pop spiritually. That should tell us all something.

So if prayer seems like an insurmountable mountain fit only for the great ascetics hidden somewhere out in the wilderness, don't buy it. Prayer is for everyone. That's why Jesus taught *all* of His disciples to pray, and it's why they intentionally recorded that prayer in the Bible. And the prayer He taught them was an everyday prayer. The words "today" and "daily bread" at least suggest that idea strongly.

This book is an invitation to join those disciples and millions of others who, down through the centuries, have taken Jesus at His Word. Once you pray this prayer with a sincere heart things are set in motion by God that only He can do! Praying what is historically called the Lord's Prayer will change your life. It will open up vistas of spiritual insight that you would otherwise never see. It will strengthen and deepen your relationship with God. It will break the dark influences on your soul. It will get you off the dead-end road of selfishness and onto the superhighway of His kingdom.

So what are we waiting for? Let's dive into this divine prayer and see what we can learn together. Let's discover the awesome life God has for us on a daily basis. Let's cast off the mundane clothes of ritual and religiousness and find the genuine relationship God has always wanted with us. It's all found in the Lord's Prayer!

CHAPTER 1

Our Father

Our Father in heaven, hallowed be your name.

Using the Word *Awesome*

One of the tragedies of this generation we are living in is an almost complete dissolution of sacredness. The concept of reverence has been replaced by sarcasm, suspicion, and mockery. Just view any newscast, read any newspaper, watch any sitcom, or listen to any radio commentator. On the other side of that equation is Jesus, who taught us to pray, "Our

Father . . . *hallowed* be Your name." It's that hallowedness I'm asking you to think about with me for a few minutes. But instead of hallowed, or reverent, or sacred, let's use the word *awesome* because it's so much more easily understood in this generation.

In 1997, Reeve Lindbergh, daughter of aviator Charles Lindbergh, was invited to give the annual Lindbergh Address at the Smithsonian Institution's Air and Space Museum to commemorate the 70th anniversary of her father's historic solo flight across the Atlantic. On the day of the speech, museum officials invited her to come early, before the facility opened, so she could have a close look at *The Spirit of St. Louis,* the little plane—suspended from the museum ceiling—that her father had piloted from New York to Paris in 1927.

That morning in the museum, Reeve and her young son, Ben, eagerly climbed into the bucket of a cherry picker, a long-armed crane that carried them upward until the plane was at eye level and within their reach. Seeing the machine that her father had so bravely flown across the sea was an unforgettable experience for Reeve. She had never touched the plane before, and that morning, 20 feet above the floor of the museum, she tenderly reached out to run her fingers along the door handle, which she knew her father must have grasped many times with his own hand.

Tears welled up in her eyes at the thought of what she was doing. "Oh, Ben," she whispered, her voice trembling, "isn't this amazing?"

"Yeah," Ben replied, equally impressed. "I've never been in a cherry picker before!"

Sounds like something Bart Simpson would say. That little guy was oblivious to the sacredness of the moment. He wasn't a bad kid, just unconscious of what was really happening. And what he was missing did matter because it had the possibility of deepening his sense of history, his relationship with his mom, and his own ability to recognize what was really important.

Have you ever heard of a little, bestselling book called *The Prayer of Jabez?* I think that little book was a stroke of genius from heaven. Bruce Wilkerson's sincere description of how a single thread of daily prayer has changed his life is truly a masterpiece of spiritual simplicity. And, though he has taken a significant amount of heat from Christians about that book because of its vulnerability to the consumer mentality, there is no question in my mind that Wilkerson's motives and message are born out of a right spirit. They are both laced with God's goodness.

But that's not all there is to prayer or God. There is so much more. *The Prayer of Jabez* is simply a wonderful and fruitful beginning point. But the prayer of Jesus, the Lord's Prayer, can take us beyond Jabez to the infinite realms of God's power and purpose for our lives. It will lead us further into an awesome life!

It Is Awesome to Have God as Our Father

More than 150 times in the gospels, Jesus used the word *Father* to convey a more accurate image of God. If we accept the fact that we were created in the image of God, then image *is* everything! Though this was not an entirely new concept to the Hebrew mind (they considered themselves children of Abraham and, through that connection, children of God), the intimacy Jesus injected into it was definitely new and even intimidating. The Jews were not even allowed to pronounce the name of God. To them it was a much more sacred concept than anything we can relate to in this generation. So for Jesus to teach that God was an intimate being who wanted to be close and personal with His people was way outside the box.

But that's what Jesus taught His disciples to pray. And it was the first and most important point. Prayer then is first about being in, and being aware of, the presence of our Father. Prayer is about seeking His face or favor long before it is anything else.

So make up your mind that, for you, praying will always be about the connection between you and your Father in heaven. If that matter isn't settled up front, the rest of the prayer will unfortunately be tainted by a consumer view of God. Prayer will turn out to be not much more than pulling the arm of a slot machine in Vegas. It will be about putting in your time and expecting a miraculous answer to come out. There's nothing really awesome about that—nothing at all.

The fact that Jesus taught a fisherman, a lawyer, a political science major, and an IRS agent that God wanted to be their father was absolutely a paradigm-breaker for that time. And for many people it still is. Don't let it be that way for you. Your Father is only waiting for you to hear Jesus' prayer and pray it. He's always been there for you, waiting for the moment when you would want to know Him as

He really is . . . your Father! What an awesome reality! The greatest person in the universe wants to hear *you,* wants you to know Him like He already knows you! Is that awesome or what?

Connections in Heaven

Jesus makes the point of defining our Father as being in heaven. No doubt there were many reasons for that purposeful statement. Let me give you just two. First, we all need to be able to distinguish our Father in heaven from our fathers on earth. There is a natural confusion about our identity that is wrapped up in our relationships with our earthly fathers and other father (or authority) figures.

On the inside, we are like ducks. When ducks are born they follow the first image they see and believe it to be their mother. It's called imprinting. They are so image-conscious right from the start. In the same way, from very early on in life we receive impressions that stick with us and become the grid through which we see life.

If one of our parents, or another authority figure, constantly tells us that we aren't measuring up, we begin to relate to life as a failure no matter how much we accomplish. That condemning image and deafening voice automatically transfer over into our relationship with God unless we do something about it. The fact that our Father is in heaven is meant to (over the course of many daily prayers) wash out those other images and replace them with the real image we are made in. If we don't allow these changes to take place, we continue to relate to our Father falsely, and that keeps confusion in our relationship. It also keeps us from enjoying and exercising a life of daily prayer. Who wants to talk every day to someone we believe doesn't like us in the first place?

As my dear friend Jerry Cook loves to say, "God is not just a bigger version of us." That would be a frightening prospect indeed. But if we're honest and thoughtful, that is often how we view the Lord. When the Cowardly Lion in *The Wizard of Oz* sang those famous words, "If I were king of the forest," the implication was that he would be a wonderful, benevolent king. But in the real world, if you or I were God, the results would be disastrous. And the results are equally disastrous spiritually when you or I create God in our image or allow Him to be tied to the image of any other being. He's not just a bigger version of your earthly father, mother, uncle, coach, or teacher.

That's why Jesus taught His disciples to pray, "Our Father *in heaven.*" That prayer was intended to move them and us away from any comparisons, because no one can compare to our Father in heaven. And failing to make that distinction seriously hampers our ability to grow heavenward or to experience the awesome things He has for us on a daily basis, because those lingering false images cloud everything.

Secondly, the fact that the Father we pray to is *in* heaven suggests that all of the things that we know about heaven come with the package. Think about how heaven might affect us every day if we really open up to it. In heaven there is perfect love. In heaven there is joy all day long. In heaven every creature praises our Father from his own perspective, voluntarily and spontaneously. In heaven everyone is provided for completely. No one is ever alone in heaven. And the list goes on, *ad infinitum.* When we pray to our Father *in heaven,* we buy into all that heaven contains. It's a veritable feast for the soul! And it's all available on a daily basis!

Someone said it best: "He who kneels before God can stand before anyone." If God is your Father, then you certainly need not cower before anyone on earth or in heaven. You are His child if you have come to know Him through the forgiveness that Christ brought when He died on the cross for you. Why would you then fear anyone or anything in this life? It's that understanding Jesus wants us to capture when we pray to "our Father in heaven."

Reverence for His Name

Hallowing our Father's name certainly involves growing in our understanding and application of His name, not using it tritely or irreverently. But it has to do with more than that. It means to honor His name by the way you live your life because you are called by His name. When Jesus was pressed to describe this reverence, He used that opportunity to encompass all of life into one single point of understanding: "Love the Lord your God with all your heart and with all your soul and with all your mind. This is the first and greatest commandment" (Matthew 22:37).

This love for "your God" (a term of personal relationship and intimacy) is all-encompassing. It's as though a daughter were to recognize that she represents her father's name and reputation when she goes to school or the grocery store or the playground. It's about a son having real respect for the family name because he loves his father and the family so much. Here is how one commentator translates this part of the Lord's Prayer:

> Let Thy name be celebrated, venerated, and esteemed as holy everywhere, and receive from all people proper honor. It is thus the expression of a wish or desire, on the part of the worshipper, that the name of God, or that God Himself, should be held everywhere in proper veneration.[1]

In other words, hearts that really love God are not just concerned about their own view of Him but how the whole world views Him. That's what the Lord's Prayer produces when you pray it sincerely. You become more and more a God person, honoring Him in your daily activities.

You need to pray that way every day. It sets the stage for all your other prayers and the rhythm for your life for that day. It destroys the sarcasm and bitterness that can so easily steal the day away from you. Take a minute and ask your Father for that reverence now!

The Balance of Life

Jerry Bridges, in his book *The Joy of Fearing God,* describes the healthy tension between loving and fearing God:

> In the physical realm there are two opposing forces called "centrifugal" and "centripetal." Centrifugal force tends to pull away from a center of rotation, while centripetal force pulls toward the center. A stone whirled about on the end of a string exerts centrifugal force on the string while the string exerts centripetal force on the stone. Take away one and the other immediately disappears. These two opposing forces can help us understand something of the fear of God. The

> centrifugal force represents the attributes of God such as his holiness and sovereignty that cause us to bow in awe and self-abasement before him. They hold us reverently distant from the one who, by the simple power of his word, created the universe out of nothing. The centripetal force represents the love of God. It surrounds us with grace and mercy and draws us with cords of love into the Father's warm embrace. To exercise a proper fear of God we must understand and respond to both these forces.[2]

That's it! When you pray "Our Father in heaven" every day, you fortify that balance in your soul. You take a stance against the arrogant attitude that seeks to elevate you above your Father and treat Him with a callousness or casualness of heart. At the same time, you deepen your love for and understanding of Him as your Father. That balance enables you to live each day in the power and humility of Christ. And that's an awesome way to live!

Reverence is the result of knowledge and trust in someone greater than you. Without that reverence, any relationship will begin to degenerate into something of less value. And this first part of the prayer that Jesus taught His disciples to pray builds reverence into your soul on a daily basis.

Exercising the Awesome Life

So start right now. Don't wait till the end of the book to start praying. Don't worry about the whole prayer. If you get this part of it down, you'll already be living in the expectancy of His awesome nature. In fact, most of us could stand to just pray this part of the Lord's Prayer for weeks before moving on. There's no hurry. If you know the Lord, eternal life has already begun for you.

Wherever you are, just begin to think about your Father in heaven. Deal with the false images in your soul with His help. Acknowledge your misconceptions. Ask Him for a better understanding of who He is. Look in the Bible and find the names for God. Each of them reveals a different aspect of His character. Just pick one and focus on it. Your Father is all of that and more.

And in this quiet time, commit yourself to talk to your Father on a daily basis, if at all possible, first thing in the morning. That gets your day started on the right foot and opens your heart to the possibilities He has for you in that day. Once you start the day thinking about and talking to your Father, everything starts looking up. That doesn't mean everything will be peachy-keen today, that nothing will go wrong for you. That would be heaven, and you're not there yet or you wouldn't be reading this book. It means that no matter what happens, you are prepared for it and equipped to handle it because you've already established who you are and who your Father is. That's enough to get you through any day!

CHAPTER 2

The Kingdom

Your kingdom come, your will be done on earth as it is in heaven.

Born for a Wonderful Life

Everyone knows the Christmas classic *It's a Wonderful Life*, starring Jimmy Stewart as a man who's lost his appreciation for life and rediscovers it through the help of an angel.

You were born for a wonder-filled life too. The Bible says that before the worlds were formed, He thought of you, knew you would exist, and planned for you to know Him. It also says that while you were being formed in your mother's womb, He was there with you, forming you for His glory. So the way you are is perfect for who He wants you to be. If that bothers you, be comforted by the fact that you'll receive another body when this life is over. But I hope you don't waste the one you have now.

I thought for years, as a child, that being short was a disadvantage. Now I know it is *my* advantage because God formed me for His glory. Being short allows me to say things to people that a tall person might not be able to say, to go places a tall person might not be able to go, and to do things a tall person might not be able to do. I love it when people who've heard me on the radio meet me in person and say, "I didn't realize you were so short." To me, that's a compliment.

Of course, my thoughts about height are not prejudicial. The same possibilities are true for a tall person, or ugly person, or any other kind of person. What you are isn't better or worse than anyone else—unless you let it be. Once I recognized that amazing truth, it set me free to have a wonder-filled life on earth with my Father in heaven.

What is keeping you from that awesome (wonderful) life? Simple. Seeking self-fulfillment and satisfaction without God. Remember, you were made for *His* glory and *His* image. Looking for fulfillment in yourself is like a dog chasing her tail. You'll never get there. It's not until we spend our days really and fully seeking God's will that we find incredible, awesome fulfillment because that's where it is temporally and eternally. That's why Jesus taught His disciples to pray, "Your kingdom come, your will be done on earth as it is in heaven." Keep reading. I'll show you what I mean.

Finding That Better Life

All of us are born with a desire for "the good life." But even the best life we can come up with falls short of a life filled with God, His ideas, and His plans. His is the better life. In other words, when it comes to life, what you don't know really can hurt you because you can end up missing out on what the great apostle Paul called the "more excellent way" (1 Corinthians 12:31). What I have to share with you is really all about surrender, but not surrender to just anything. It is about surrender to the better life. In the Bible God says, "My thoughts are not your thoughts, neither are your ways my ways . . . as the heavens are higher than the earth, so are my ways higher than your ways and my thoughts than your thoughts" (Isaiah 55:8).

That's why Jesus taught His disciples to pray for His kingdom to come. He knew our attempts to establish our own little fiefdoms would never match His!

Some folks say that Jesus did not have a very good life. He was born into what was probably a less-than-affluent family, never gained much wealth, lived a relatively obscure childhood even though His gifts were beyond genius, was often and unjustly misunderstood as an adult, was betrayed by His best friends, had all of our guilt dumped on Him by our heavenly Father, and ultimately was killed by the people He came to help. Does that sound like Jimmy Stewart's wonderful life to you? And yet, here is what Jesus had to say about His own life. "These things I have spoken to you, that my joy may remain in you, and that your joy might be full" (John 15:11).

Does that sound to you like someone who's having a miserable life? What is this great joy that He wants to be complete in our lives—that He wants to fill us up with? It is *His* joy! It is the joy of a life that is filled with all that heaven has to offer. A kingdom is the place where a king rules. God's kingdom is the place where He rules. It can be as far-reaching as the farthest solar system from our planet or as near as your heart. But wherever He rules, all of the attributes of heaven are available. And that's definitely a better life, an awesome life. It's a life that can overcome anything in this life.

Finding Life in His Work

When Jesus teaches us to pray for our Father's kingdom to come, He talks about the external things of life, about what happens on the outside of us. The Scriptures tell us that the "increase of His government and peace will know no end" (Isaiah 9:7). It is that government that He wants us to pray for. This is about surrendering what you see (the circumstances) to your Father in Heaven and wanting God's kind of actions to take place today right where you live, work, and play.

The obvious implication is that this prayer isn't just a smattering of things we hope will happen but a search for what we think God wants to do where we are . . . through us. It's not a rote recitation of some magical formula, but a mystical discovery of what God is up to and an ironclad agreement with His will.

Mychal F. Judge was a Franciscan friar and Fire Department chaplain who died in the World Trade Center attack. He wrote and carried in his pocket a prayer that is dear to the firemen in New York and famous around the world. It is known to the firemen as Mychal's prayer:

> Lord, take me where you want me to go.
> Let me meet who you want me to meet.
> Tell me what you want me to say. And
> keep me out of your way.[3]

That's a prayer about God's work! That's the kind of thing Jesus was after when He taught His disciples to pray for God's kingdom to come. Have you asked God how He wants His kingdom to come in your home, in the place where you work, in your neighborhood, or in your community?

Before becoming a pastor, I worked as a respiratory therapist, and I asked God every day for His kingdom to come. In response,

He told me to show up to work before my co-workers and pray for them individually. Every day I got opportunities to share His love with them, and over time they each asked me to pray for them. Some gave their hearts to Christ. But even those who didn't showed a reverence for Him. It was an awesome experience!

That's just one small example of an answer to the prayer "Your kingdom come." Imagine what God might ask you to do today. The possibilities are limitless. And they all work because He's behind them. His kingdom is unstoppable. It will never end. And you've signed up for the duration! Ask Him to show you the work He has planned for you. Be a part of the expansion of His kingdom today!

Finding Life in His Will

This is the internal part of the prayer. It is about your will and God's. It's about who will win that battle today. It was the same battle Jesus fought in the wilderness, at the beginning of His ministry, and in the garden just before the cross. Even Jesus had to pray *until* He completely surrendered His will to His Father. Who are we to think that we don't need to pray this prayer and mean it? It is reasonable to assume that Jesus prayed that way every day in between. That explains why He, in the most crushing moment of his life, was able to stand in the shadow of the cross and say yes. He taught His disciples to pray the very same way. Again, this is not about relinquishing your will to nothing. That's Eastern mysticism: your individual will blending into the great nothingness. This prayer is about yielding to something and someone greater!

This part of the Lord's prayer must come after "Our Father." Otherwise, it is a lifeless call to obedience without any sense of real love or reward. Here is how the great commentator Alexander MacLaren put it:

> If men begin with the will, then their religion will be slavish, a dull, sullen resignation, or a painful, weary round of unwelcome duties and reluctant abstaining. The will of an unknown God will be in their thoughts a dark and tyrannous necessity, a mysterious, inscrutable force, which rules by virtue of being stronger, and demands only obedience. There is no more horrible conception of God than that which makes Him merely or mainly sovereign will.[4]

But, as he goes on to say, if we consider the Father who made the beauty of creation, the complexity of the human body, and the enormity of His name and Word, then the whole view of obedience becomes something entirely different. Then our surrender, "instead of being slavish is filial; instead of being reluctant submission to a mightier force, is glad conformity to the fountain of love and goodness; instead of being sullen resignation, is trustful reliance; instead of being painful execution of unwelcome duties, is spontaneous expression in acts which are [born] of indwelling love."[5]

This is an everyday need for every human being. Don't be afraid to let go and allow God to be your everything. He will only do you good. He's the only one who loved you before you were conceived. And He's the only one you can be sure will love you at the end of the day. Finding His will is an awesome place of security, healing, and love. If you fall, He will pick you up. If you fail, He will forgive you. Your will is dangerous and treacherous at best. His will is eternally predictable!

Finding Life in His Way

In a very real sense, this is the final point of surrender—because His way of doing things often does not fit into our matrix of options. "On earth as it is in heaven" has very specific implications. There are no committees in heaven, only obedient servants. In heaven, all the attention is on the throne. In heaven, the atmosphere is full of praise. Unstoppable, holy enthusiasm for our Father laces everyone's attitude. Hope, peace, and love are in everyone's hearts. This part of the prayer is about what you project out of your life, the *way* His will gets done. It's about the way you do things today.

We all have our way of doing things. Some of that is good. It's the unique way He made us. For example, I'm left-handed; that's my way of writing and doing things. But some of the things we do are not good at all—such as when a person uses sulking as a means of manipulation to get his way. Our Father wants to change those ways to His ways.

In the Old Testament, the great leader Joshua put it this way: "Choose this day whom you will serve."[6] Don't just choose God—choose His way!

Finding Those Points of Yielding

Near the end of *It's a Wonderful Life*, George Bailey (Jimmy Stewart) has an epiphany and declares that he sees what God wants to do. Joyfully, he decides, "I can do it!" That statement is followed with a big "*Yes!*" He realizes that the life God has for him is better than all the things he had been worrying about; that it will all work out if he just yields his soul to God.

I remember a moment in my life much like George Bailey's. For two years, I pursued my ex-girlfriend, Susan, trying to convince her to be my wife. But because I had hurt her so deeply once before, she flatly rejected my every offer. Then I found Christ. Actually, Susan found Him first and introduced me to the idea of following Him. After some serious resistance of my own, I surrendered and gave my life to Jesus. But I still wanted Susan to be my wife. Then one day the Holy Spirit, who had just moved into my life, told me it was time to surrender that hope to Him. Like George Bailey—who saw how hopeless his family and friends would be without him—I could not imagine life without Susan. There were moments in my life when I felt that I would suffocate without her. But as I listened to the Lord, a new peace swept over my spirit. As a new Christian, I heard the Lord whisper in my heart, "I'll be there for you. And what I have to offer you will be better than anything you can do for yourself." Somehow, by the grace of God, I yielded my heart and gave up Susan to Him. I said to Him, "If this relationship is not for me, then I know with Your love I'll be OK." I surrendered to His kingdom (His outward plan) and His will (His inward plan) for my life.

The rest is history. Within a week the woman who once swore she would never be mine proposed to me! We were married a week later, and here we are today thirty-one years later (as of this writing) still happily married. I still cannot imagine life without her. But the good news is that I found out I could make it either way. God's love in my life would make up for whatever absence of love I might have to contend with in the world. That's what surrender does. It puts you in a win-win situation. It gives you *the* better life!

Exercising His Kingdom

What is God asking you to surrender today? The first and obvious answer is your will. But don't let your prayer stop there. Be specific. What is your Father asking you to let go of so He can have His way? Is there something in your heart that you have not yielded to Him yet? Is there some situation at work you need to ask Him about? Are you battling alone with a problem at home? Is your world too myopic—do you find yourself always thinking of your own problems with no concern for the world around you? Don't go any further with this book. Take the time right now to surrender your will. Take the time to ask the Lord what His work is for you. Your Father has so many things He wants to show you about the world around you and about your inner world. He's waiting for you to ask. Surrender, and pray for *the* better life!

CHAPTER 3

Praying for God's Provision

Give us today our daily bread.

Asking for Satisfaction

One of the biggest early hits of the Rolling Stones was a song called "Satisfaction." The key line in the refrain is "I can't get no satisfaction." In some ways it is the theme of the baby boomer generation that ultimately produced the consumer society we live in right now.

Jesus has a different song to sing. The song of His heart is all about the satisfaction that *can* be found in our Father in heaven. So Jesus taught His disciples to ask for God's provision every day. Clearly, He wasn't asking us to beg for bread. He was very aware of His own word in the Psalms: "I was young, and now I am old, yet I have never seen the righteous forsaken or their children begging bread" (Psalm 37:25).

Instead, Jesus teaches us to connect every day with our Father about His provision so we do not fall into the trap of *dis*satisfaction, seeking help from every other avenue. "Daily bread" isn't just about today. It's also about being satisfied with enough. And this might be the most important time in this generation to know when enough is enough.

John Ortberg wrote in an article in *Leadership Today:*

> When we take our children to the shrine of the Golden Arches, they always lust for the meal that comes with a cheap little prize, a combination christened, in a mo-

ment of marketing genius, the Happy Meal. You're not just buying fries, McNuggets, and a dinosaur stamp; you're buying happiness. Their advertisements have convinced my children they have a little McDonald-shaped vacuum in their souls: "Our hearts are restless till they find their rest in a Happy Meal." I try to buy off the kids sometimes. I tell them to order only the food and I'll give them a quarter to buy a little toy on their own. But the cry goes up, "I want a Happy Meal." All over the restaurant, people crane their necks to look at the tight-fisted, penny-pinching cheapskate of a parent who would deny a child the meal of great joy.

The problem with the Happy Meal is that the happy wears off, and they need a new fix. No child discovers lasting happiness in just one: "Remember that Happy Meal? What great joy I found there." Happy Meals bring happiness only to McDonald's. You ever wonder why Ronald

> McDonald wears that grin? Twenty billion Happy Meals, that's why. When you get older, you don't get any smarter; your happy meals just get more expensive.[7]

Jesus has a better idea that He taught His disciples and us to pray—the Lord's Prayer. He taught us to pray that we get smarter and recognize what fuels the real fire of happiness. He taught us to pray for satisfaction by recognizing and praying for our daily needs. That's the focus of this chapter.

Ask for Provision

I recently received an e-mail about a 6-year old girl in our church who prayed for her dead pet (a frog), and he came back to life. That little girl has tremendous faith! When her father asked her about it, she said, "I have a lot of faith and that's why my frog came back to life. It took Lazarus three days, but my frog came back in only one!" Most of us are on the other end of that idea, allowing our disappointments to make us cautious in asking.

There is a lot wrapped up in this simple idea of asking. For instance, the concept that God actually *wants* to provide for us is difficult for many to grasp. As children, many of us learned that asking was a "wear them down" experience. As a result of those experiences, the sense of distraction or reluctance manifested by our parents is transferred to God. But throughout His whole ministry, Jesus portrays our Father in an entirely different way. He said, "If you, being evil [in comparison to God], know how to give good gifts to your children, how much more will your heavenly Father give the Spirit to those who ask Him?"

On the other hand, in another place, Jesus describes an older brother who perceived his father as reluctant to give:

> But he answered his father, "Look! All these years I've been slaving for you and never disobeyed your orders. Yet you never gave me even a young goat so I could celebrate with my friends. But when this son of yours who has squandered your property with prostitutes comes home, you kill the fattened calf for him."
> "My son," the father said, "you are always with me, and everything I have is yours." (Luke 15:29–31)

Apparently, this older son never asked. He made assumptions about his father without even asking. The result cost him years of confusion and pain. Asking is about remaining childlike in our relationship with our Father in heaven. But are we just supposed to ask for ourselves? Jesus said, "Give us . . .," and that leads me to the next point.

Ask for Us

Throughout this whole prayer, but certainly in this verse, it is important not to overlook the plural pronouns Jesus used in teaching His disciples about prayer. Using *us* and *our* lifts our view of provision out of the self-consumed mode of the individual and into the glorious height of a heaven-bound community called "the saints." This is not the spirit of communism but the spirit of community—the desire to always have our brothers and sisters in mind as we enjoy the fruits of our own labors. Here's what Moses had to say: "Do not go over your vineyard a second time or pick up the grapes that have fallen. Leave them for the poor and alien" (Leviticus 19:10).

God taught His people this principle in the Old Testament and Jesus confirmed it in the New Testament. Remembering the needy as we ask for our own bread each day is not an option. It's a part of God's way of life for *us*.

Ask Today

The idea of today is a powerful concept throughout God's Word. The word is used over 200 times in the Bible. God wants our relationship with Him to be fresh. He wants the things He does for us, in us, and through us to be new—like the dew upon the grass.

"Today," Paul says in Hebrews 4, "if you hear His voice do not harden your hearts." Today is the most important day of your life because you no longer have yesterday and tomorrow may not come. When it comes to our needs (Matthew 6:33), God doesn't want us to think much beyond today. Today is about priorities; it's about relationships. A dull heart today can mean a distant heart tomorrow. But what are we to ask for? The answer is . . .

Ask for Today's Needs

God doesn't want us to be so "provided for" that we lose the urgent sense of need in our lives. And in direct connection with the principle of provision, Jesus taught His disciples *not* to worry about provision, but instead to concentrate on God's character and kingdom as the priority. So daily bread (need) is really about daily character, about a gut-check of what really matters. Jesus had John write a letter to a church once about this, saying, "You say, 'I am rich; I have acquired wealth and do not need a thing.' But you do not realize that you are wretched, poor, pitiful, blind, and naked" (Revelation 3:17–18).

If you're not in need today, surely someone around you is. And because we are all created in God's image, others' needs become our needs too! That's "us"! When we ask our Father for bread, He will not give us a stone. That's why He wants us to ask. By asking Him, we invite His provision and the supernatural into today!

God's Provision through Us

John Rosemond, a funny nationally syndicated columnist—and also a family psychologist—likes to take unusual informal polls of parents. Whenever he's in a foreign culture, he asks parents, "Do your kids complain about boredom?" Without exception everyone outside of this country answers him "no." In fact, parents in other cultures look at him with incredulity, as if to say, "Boredom and kids just don't go together!"

Rosemond also questions parents who raised their kids in the forties and fifties. He asks, "When you were raising your kids back then, did you hear them complain about boredom?" The typical response is "Rarely."

In another of his little surveys, Rosemond asks middle-aged parents, "How many toys did you have growing up?" The answers range from zero to ten, but mostly these folks respond with something like, "Toys? We took a cardboard box, and we made something out of it." In contrast, Rosemond says the typical American child of five years of age has accumulated two hundred fifty toys! Now, since five-year-olds have only lived for two hundred sixty weeks, they're apparently accumulating almost one new toy per week—and they're bored!

What if as children of the Lord, we ask Him for *gifts* instead of toys each day? That would create a much bigger and better world for us than just trying to get God to give us what we want for ourselves today. Imagine what God could do through us if we just asked!

Exercising His Provision

Stop and think about it right now. Is there something you can ask God to provide that would be a blessing for you or someone else? Are there people around you out of work? Pray for them. Is there someone in your family in need of something? Pray for her. Do you know someone at work who is barely getting by? Pray for him.

Make a list of those in need around you. And don't confine those needs only to financial or material things. There may be someone in close proximity to you who needs a big dose of God's love. Pray for that person. Then be ready to be the answer if it is within your grasp.

If you practice this type of prayer on a daily basis, God will show you needs you were previously unable or unwilling to see. He will open your eyes to the world of need around you and empower you in miraculous ways to meet those needs. God has the answer to every human need. He's waiting only for His people to ask.

Meeting another human being's need is the most satisfying thing in life. It puts you in touch with God's will and His way. It is the natural prayer to pray after asking for His kingdom to come. It is where the real joy is—the joy of an awesome life!

CHAPTER 4

Freedom

Forgive us our debts, as we have forgiven our debtors.

Praying for a Life of Freedom

Forgiveness is about freedom. There is no freedom on the outside without real freedom on the inside. Martin Luther King, Jr. understood that well. He had a dream about freedom. But his dream could not be realized without first achieving freedom from the fear of pain and death. Dr. King was no masochist. He simply lived in freedom from people's opinions and actions. That kind of freedom cannot be purchased. But there is definitely a way to find it.

C. S. Lewis was one of the great writers of the 20th century. In his book *Mere Christianity,* here's what he had to say about forgiveness and freedom:

> I remember Christian teachers telling me long ago that I must hate a bad man's actions, but not hate the bad man: or, as they would say, hate the sin but not the sinner. For a long time I used to think this a silly, straw-splitting distinction: how could you hate what a man did and not hate the man? But years later it occurred to me that there was one man to whom I had been doing this all my life—namely myself.
>
> However much I might dislike my own cowardice or conceit or greed, I went on loving myself. There had never been the slightest difficulty about it. In fact the very reason why I hated the things was that I

> loved the man. Just because I loved myself, I was sorry to find that I was the sort of man who did those things.
>
> Consequently, Christianity does not want us to reduce by one atom the hatred we feel for cruelty and treachery. We ought to hate them. Not one word of what we have said about them needs to be unsaid. But it does want us to hate them in the same way in which we hate things in ourselves: being sorry that the man should have done such things, and hoping, if it is anyway possible, that somehow, sometime, somewhere, he can be cured and made human again.[8]

Like C. S. Lewis, all of us need freedom from the failures of others if we are going to be effective followers of Jesus Christ. Do you ever have trouble letting go of your own mistakes or the mistakes of others? Everyone does. That's why Jesus made forgiveness one of the big five subjects to be covered regularly, perhaps daily, in prayer.

In our neighborhood there is a business that does its advertising by putting a small paper ad in a small plastic bag. They throw the bag onto each driveway, knowing that people have to pick them up in order to keep their driveways clean. The secret to these advertising bags is the rocks placed inside. The rocks provide enough weight for the bag to be tossed effectively onto the driveway and stay there. The funny thing is that the rocks actually take up more space than the ad.

I thought to myself once, "What if I just left those bags in my driveway and never picked them up? That would teach those advertisers!" But after a little thought, I realized that ultimately, I would be the loser. Those bags would just pile up until I started tripping over them. On top of that, they would quickly become an eyesore to all of my neighbors. No one would actually notice them at first. But eventually they would become intolerable.

That's what it's like when we don't live in the freedom of forgiveness. Unforgiven acts, like the rocks, just pile up in our hearts. Imagine yourself walking around with your pockets or your purse filled with rocks every day. The irritation would drive you mad and probably make you edgy with everyone around you. Again, that's what unforgiveness is like. Let's look a little closer at this part of the Lord's Prayer and I'll show you what I mean.

Forgiveness Is about Freedom from Debt

Interestingly, when Luke describes this prayer of Jesus, he uses the word "sin" instead of "debts." I guess Jesus' disciples considered the terms interchangeable. But most of us don't think of sin that way. We often don't recognize the powerful aftereffects of sin, not only in our own lives but the lives of others. Every sin that gets committed is like the accrual of another debt. Something is lost. And a sense of guilt begins to lurk just under the surface of our personalities. Have you ever been in serious debt, or have you known someone who was? Do you remember what it felt like? You wake up with a pit in your stomach. You don't want to answer the phone. People don't know why you're so tense. Maybe you don't even know. That's what unforgiveness—or unconfessed sin—feels like.

One day, as Jesus sent His disciples out to love people, He said to them, "Freely you have received, freely give." That's what He says in teaching us to pray this prayer. Of course, the assumption is that you are receiving freely. Here's how Jesus said it in another place: "But he who has been forgiven little loves little" (Luke 7:47b).

Well, you can't get any more straightforward than that. Having trouble loving? Perhaps it is because you are having trouble receiving forgiveness. Jesus wants you and me to receive all of the forgiveness God has to offer every day. He doesn't want us walking around with rocks in our pockets, affecting the way we feel about life and making us react harshly to others around us.

A Lesson on Forgiveness and Debt

I learned this lesson the hard way one day. I was a young pastor with only two other employees beside myself working for the church. One of those employees was my assistant pastor; the other was a secretary. It was Friday and I had given the secretary the day off so she could go with the women of our church to our first annual women's retreat.

A few days earlier I told the assistant pastor, at his discretion, to do some shopping for the church in a nearby town. I told him he could choose the day and time. Of course, he picked Friday. What both he and I forgot was that a brochure was to accompany the women to their retreat. Someone would have to do that brochure by 11 A.M. that day, and it was now 9:30 A.M. Translation: I would have to do it. And my graphics abilities have never been my strong suit. It was a disaster in the making.

After a few feeble attempts at doing the brochure, I became quite frustrated and began to pace up and down the office hallway, muttering to myself about how my assistant had let me down by picking that day to do the shopping. I said things like "That's just like him." Then I began to remember other things about him that frustrated me.

Pacing up and down in the hallway is way out of character for me. I'm normally a fairly calm person in almost any setting. But there were rocks building up in my driveway. Eventually I found myself at the back door of the church, fuming with frustration, and I did something I've never done before or since. I kicked the door with all of my might. Thank goodness it was a metal door and only my foot was damaged.

After whining briefly over the pain in my foot, I began to walk away from the door, and something strange happened. I felt the equivalent of a hand on my chest. As quickly as I felt that hand I heard the voice of the Lord speak—not audibly, but to my heart—saying, "I want you to forgive that man."

You're not going to like this, but I laughed. I honestly thought the Lord was kidding. In my arrogance I was convinced the Lord knew my assistant like I did and couldn't possibly be pleased with him either. So I proceeded to walk on.

Again I felt a heavy hand on my chest forcing me to stop in my tracks. And again I heard the Lord speak to my heart. This time the tone was different. I realized He was not requesting my obedience but demanding it. "I said I want you to forgive that man *right now!*" He said.

All of a sudden I began to cry uncontrollably because I realized that I could not obey, and I had never found myself in that position before. Don't get me wrong. I've disobeyed God's commandments many times, but never when He spoke to me in such a direct manner. I was dumbfounded and frightened.

I quickly responded to the Lord, "I don't understand. Why would You ask me to do something I cannot do? I can't control my feelings about this man. I can't change what I feel inside. So if You want me to forgive him You'll have to show me how." I knew God loved me but I also knew this was a big, big moment in my life.

As quickly as I asked for help, the Lord responded. He said, "How many times have you sinned against Me?" And immediately my life flashed before my eyes. I was not a Christian until the age of 22, and my life before that was filled with wrong things. I was seeing awful things that I had done, hearing words that I had said, and even remembering things I had thought that were against God. It was brutal. So I rounded off the number and said, "I don't know Lord . . . I guess about a million."

But the Lord was so gracious. He asked, "What do you owe Me for all of those sins you committed against Me?"

"Nothing," I said. "I don't owe You anything because You've forgiven me for everything through the sacrifice of Your son Jesus on the cross."

Then the Lord pulled a fast one on me. He said, "And how many times has this man sinned against you?" The horrible truth is that a number came to mind immediately, because I had been rehearsing my frustrations about this man only a few minutes earlier one by one. So I responded, "I think seventeen or eighteen."

Well, it didn't take a genius to do the math at that point. God was willing to forgive me for a million things I'd said and done and thought that were so wrong. But I could not let go of 17 or 18 things that I thought this guy did to me.

Suddenly the world of unforgiveness as indebtedness opened up to me. I understood that for most of my life, I felt that my wife owed me a kiss and a good meal when I came home from work. I'd never said that to her but it was in my heart. And I understood that my kids owed me A's on their report cards because they were my children, preacher's kids. I'd never said that to them but it was in my heart. And sadly I understood that my whole congregation owed me the expectation of showing up every weekend to hear my great messages. I'd never said that to them, but it was in my heart. I was painfully aware, in a way that I had never noticed before, that everyone owed me something. Very few people would have seen me that way, but God saw my heart and was kind enough to save me from myself.

So, even though I did not fully feel the impact of this equation yet, I pronounced my forgiveness. I said, "This guy doesn't owe me anything." Then I went further and announced to the Lord, "I don't want anyone to owe me anything—my wife, my children, the congregation, or anyone else." It was an amazing, exhilarating feeling!

I was so emotionally and spiritually high from the feeling of freedom, I began to jump up and down, something way out of character for me. I began to shout, "No one owes me anything!" I was still jumping up and down, repeating that new liberating statement, when the telephone rang. It was the guy who only a few minutes earlier had owed me for seventeen or eighteen sins.

I knew I had really forgiven him because there was no weird feeling in my gut when I heard his name on the other end of the line. I really loved him with God's love. But listen to what he said: "Pastor, you're not going to believe this, but I was just driving around doing my shopping when I heard the Lord speak to me, almost audibly, and say, 'Pull over at that phone booth, call Ron, and ask him if he needs help with anything right now.'"

Now you and I both know that if I had not forgiven him a few minutes earlier, that phone never would have rung. God was not going to talk to him about my needs until I talked to God about his need for freedom from my bitterness. That's exactly what Jesus was getting at with this prayer of forgiveness.

Forgiveness Is about Freedom for Today

Forgiveness requires a day-to-day fight for freedom of the soul from the offenses committed by others and ourselves. It is a battle that we must win if we're going to make a difference for God in this world. And this is the only portion of the Lord's Prayer that Jesus commented on afterward. Here's what He had to say about it: "For if you forgive men when they sin against you, your heavenly Father will also forgive you. But if you do not forgive men their sins, your Father will not forgive your sins" (Matthew 6:14–15).

Whew! That must tell us something about the importance of this particular part of the prayer. Perhaps it was because Jesus knew this was the hardest part to live out consistently. That's why this prayer is clearly about daily issues.

Did you know that the annual cost of running red lights (in medical bills, car repairs, etc.) is 7 billion dollars while the average amount of time saved by running a red light is 50 seconds? You don't really save anything by rushing through life. And you don't save anything by rushing past the consequences of things that go wrong in and around you. You need to slow down and deal with things so that your heart doesn't fill up with rocks. Today is all you have. Don't hold on to your mistakes or the mistakes of others.

Forgiveness Is about Freedom for All

Remember, everything in this prayer includes "us." It's plural. Praying for a life of freedom is praying not just for your own freedom but the freedom of others as well. It is also praying that your life will bring freedom to others. Jesus looked down from the cross and said, "Father, forgive them for they do not know what they are doing" (Luke 23:34). How could He do that? They were crucifying Him. It's simple. He was the embodiment of God's love, the perfect expression of God's forgiveness. If forgiveness is a real part of your life, it works at the worst times, not just when it's easy.

The word *as,* in the prayer Jesus taught His disciples to pray, implies that you are going to do something. It's the same idea as the Great Commission in Matthew 28. The language there really means, "As you are going, make disciples of all nations." In other words, as we follow up on our commitment to handle relationships righteously, with grace and compassion, God will start His work in us at the same time. I didn't feel anything when I first said, "OK, that guy doesn't owe me anything." But once I said those words sincerely, everything kicked into gear in heaven.

The unwillingness to forgive goes all the way back to the genesis of mankind: "I have killed a man for wounding me, a young man for injuring me" (Genesis 4:23b). This ties in amazingly with the words of Jesus:

> Then Peter came to Jesus and asked, "Lord, how many times shall I forgive my brother when he sins against me? Up to seven times?" Jesus answered, "I tell you, not seven times, but seventy-seven times." (Matthew 18:21–22)

What Peter asked Jesus points all the way back to that time in history when Lamech proudly announced his revenge on the young man he killed. It was the genesis of road rage. And it is noteworthy to recognize that men began to call on God *not* out of the lineage of Cain (or Lamech) but Seth (Genesis 4:26).

Unforgiveness never just affects you individually. It always affects "us."

On the other hand, the principle and practice of forgiveness definitely provide us with one of the "keys of the kingdom" that either unleashes the power of God in our lives or causes us to "freeze up" spiritually, in much the same way that a computer locks up because of a virus. Once again, the words of Jesus: "I will give you the keys of the kingdom; whatever you bind on earth will be bound in heaven, and whatever you loose on earth will be loosed in heaven" (Matthew 16:19).

In the same way that you must respond to a virus with quickness and alertness to avoid serious damage to the hard drive of a computer, you must respond quickly and wisely to the relationships around you. That again is why I suggest Jesus meant for us to deal with this issue *daily!* He doesn't want things to pile up in our driveways.

A Metaphor for Freedom

I read somewhere the story of a town where all the residents were ducks. Every Sunday the ducks would waddle out of their houses and down the main street of their town to the only church in town. They would waddle into the meeting room and squat in their prospective pews. The duck choir would waddle in and take its place, and then the duck minister would come forward and open his duck Bible. He would read to them, "Ducks! God has given you wings! With wings you can fly! With wings you can mount up and soar like eagles. No walls can confine you! No fences can hold you! You have wings. God has given you wings, and you can fly like birds!" All the ducks shouted, "Amen!" Then they all *waddled* home unchanged.

Freedom is not a lofty ideal to be cheered. And we are not ducks. We are people made in the image of God. So freedom is an attainable goal for each day. That's why Jesus told us to pray this way . . . *every day!* It's not a law, and He won't love us any less if we miss a day. But we'll probably love a little less if we do. So it's important not to let much time go by before praying this part of the Lord's Prayer.

Exercising Freedom

OK. Now you know the key to freedom every day: Keep your heart clean from the buildup of rocks. So please stop right now and practice this prayer. Don't go another minute with your (or other people's) failures weighing you down. Go ahead. Say it. "No one owes me anything."

You're not saying that nothing happened, that offenses committed against you weren't real or didn't count. You're saying that God will take care of those things in His time, His way. And you're saying that because you know you've committed a million sins or more in your lifetime, you don't want God to take any of His forgiveness back. He's forgiven you for *everything*, if you've asked. So you don't owe Him anything for the many wrongs you've done. You're free! It would be incredibly petty to turn around and want to choke someone else for their 17 or 18 (or 100) offenses. The truth is that every time we choose to hold on to other people's offenses, we lock out the possibility of God's power intervening—the phone doesn't ring.

So say it again: "No one owes me anything." Get used to saying it every day. It will change your life forever! It will teach you the true meaning of freedom! It will teach you to live like Jesus in this world!

CHAPTER 5

Direction

And lead us not into temptation, but deliver us from the evil one.

Praying for a Life That Keeps Going in the Right Direction

The End, starring Burt Reynolds, is a classic film comedy about a man who is miserable and wants to end his life. But every time he tries to do himself in, he changes his mind at the last minute and survives. He doesn't really want to die. He's just very unhappy. Then one day he walks into the ocean, planning to drown himself. But when he gets way out into the water and realizes that he can't make it back to shore, he changes his mind and begins praying to God. His prayer, in short, is the classic prayer so many of us pray in our hour of need: "Oh God, if you get me out of this one I'll serve you for the rest of my life." And, of course, he makes it back to shore and then quickly begins to renege on the prayer of desperation he just prayed.

How many times have you heard someone pray like that, or prayed that way yourself? The amazing thing about God is that He almost always answers those prayers, because He is merciful to all. But the deceptive thing is that we may begin to believe that we can continue living that way. When that happens, we wade out into life as if we had the strength in ourselves to pull it off—when, in fact, we are wading out into our own demise.

The Archbishop of Calcutta, Henry D'Souza, knew that Mother Teresa, at times in her life, felt abandoned by God. He said that in one letter to him, she wrote that she had been walking the streets of Calcutta searching for a house where she could start her work. At the end of the day, she wrote in her diary, "I wandered the streets the whole day. My feet are aching, and I have not been able to find a home. And I also get the Tempter telling me, 'Leave all this, go back to the convent from which you came.'"

But she did not respond to the Tempter. She would not give up. And, of course, she found her home in every sense of that word. Now her Missionaries of Charity feed 500,000 families a year in Calcutta alone, treat 90,000 leprosy patients annually, and educate 20,000 children every year.

What if Mother Teresa had given up after wandering the streets and finding no real answers? What if she had believed the words of the Tempter? God would have found someone to do His work. But Mother Teresa would have missed an amazing lifetime of fulfillment that could come only through that experience. Not only would she have missed helping all those people, but many of them wouldn't be in heaven to meet her as a part of her reward. God doesn't want temptation to rob us of the destiny He has for us.

Anyone with any real sense of spiritual sensitivity will tell you that temptation is a *daily battle*, by varying degrees. But there is a way to win on a daily basis. The secret is found at the tail end of the Lord's Prayer. And though this is only my very subjective conjecture, I think it might be the last thing Jesus taught His disciples to pray for a reason. When one reads through the gospels, it's not hard to see that before receiving the power of the Holy Spirit, the disciples were not a very spiritually vigilant lot. This prayer, in the order of things, leaves us with a challenge to be vigilant every day so the Tempter does not catch us off guard. I'm sure, like me, you've noticed that he is not kind enough to announce his temptations in advance. They always seem to come out of the blue . . . unless we are prepared at the start of the day through prayer!

Wouldn't it be great if the next time life sideswiped you, you came out on top? It's simply a matter of being prepared for each day and knowing where your strength comes from. Don't pass over that statement. Don't be foolish enough to think you can navigate through the treacherous waters of today without help from above. Get in the prayer mode and get prepared for life by talking to God regularly about temptation instead of leaning on your good intentions to do better next time.

Avoidance of Temptation

Why did Jesus tell us to pray for God not to "lead us into temptation" when He was, in fact, led by the Spirit into the wilderness to be tempted? In the book of James we are told that God does not tempt anyone, but that "each one is tempted when, by his own evil desire, he is dragged away and enticed"

(James 1:14). Therefore we know God does not tempt us, nor did He tempt Jesus. But He will send us into the battle sometimes, as He sent Jesus, to test our resolve and allow us to see our spiritual condition.

First and foremost, then, "Lead us not into temptation" is about promising to follow God's leading *today*. Some time back, I experienced this in a very painful way. I'd had trouble sleeping for years. So I got a prescription for some sleeping medication. At first, it worked wonderfully. I slept soundly for the first time in a while. But two weeks later I was away on business and found myself deeply depressed for no good reason. My wife suggested that it was the medication. After recovering, I asked the Lord why this had happened, and He said, "You didn't ask Me before doing this." It wasn't that God was so insecure that He needed me to check with Him before doing things. I didn't sense anger in His voice. Rather, I sensed His disappointment in the results of my own unthinking choices. I was led into temptation by my own need. It was a powerful lesson indeed. I just wasn't praying specifically for His leading in that situation, and it cost me a sizeable amount of unnecessary confusion and pain.

"Lead us not into temptation" is also about recognizing our weakness, our absolute dependency on His leading and strength. It was not sin when Jesus, in the Garden of Gethsemane, asked His Father to remove that trial from Him, if there was any way to do so. It was an acknowledgement of His sense of weakness (having taken on the baggage of human flesh) in facing the trial that was before Him. It was the human side of Him, if you will. Jesus knew there would be times when temptation would seem unbearable. That's why He taught us to pray that way *every day*. And that leads me to the other half of this important part of the Lord's Prayer.

Deliverance from Temptation

First of all, *deliver* is a strong word in the original language that the Bible was written in. It includes the idea of an emergency rescue operation. It means to pull someone up out of a hole. Jude uses the same idea in his letter when he says, "Be merciful to those who doubt; snatch other from the fire and save them" (Jude 22–23).

That word *snatch* is the operative word. Isn't that how we all prefer it? If the Lord would just promise to pull us out of every fix we get ourselves into, then we would be free to make decisions without any concern for the ramifications.

Unfortunately, it isn't always that easy. Deliverance is nearly always a cooperative effort. As the great Apostle Paul points out in his letter to the church at Corinth, "No temptation has seized you except what is common to man. And God is faithful; he will not let you be tempted beyond what you can bear.

But when you are tempted, he will provide a way out so you can stand up under it" (1 Corinthians 10:13).

That "way of escape" is always there. But seeing or responding to it isn't always easy to do. Sometimes, as with Jesus in the Garden, the way is straight ahead, dead on through the trial. In those cases the way of escape is in your heart. It's not a question of changing the circumstances but of praying until the pressure is broken—until God's will wins out over yours.

And let's not forget that this is an "us" prayer. We are taught to pray not just for ourselves but for all of our brothers and sisters in Christ. If you take the word *me* and just turn the M upside down, you get *we*. There is a beautiful example of this in Jesus' own prayers. In fact, it would be more accurate to call this one the Lord's Prayer because it was actually one He prayed: "My prayer is not that you take them out of the world but that you protect them from the evil one" (John 17:15).

Jesus prayed for you when He spoke those words to our Father. He invites us all to join in that prayer for one another every day. Do it! You *can* make a difference in other people's lives through prayer.

Junk-Food Temptation

Leann Birch, a developmental psychologist at Pennsylvania State University, performed an experiment in which she took a large group of kids and fed them a huge lunch. Immediately after that meal she put them in a room with lots of junk food. "What we see is that some kids eat almost nothing," she said. "But other kids really chow down, and one of the things that predict how much they eat is the extent to which parents have restricted their access to high-fat, high-sugar food in the past. The more the kids have been restricted, the more they eat."

Birch's study also discovered that the children on restricted diets believed the junk food tasted good primarily because they had been told that junk food was bad for them! That's right. There was a direct correlation between being told "no" and wanting something.

Wow! Things haven't changed much since the Garden of Eden. Things that aren't really good *for* us still look, taste, and feel good *to* us. And when we know we shouldn't have something, we automatically begin to think how unfair that is. There are no new temptations, only new packages of presentation. It's an alluring world out there. So don't venture out on your own today. Pray, listen, and follow.

Exercising His Protection

Wouldn't it be great if you could walk in the confidence that Jesus walked in? It's not out of reach. He once spent forty days in Spirit-to-spirit combat with the Devil and came out in the power of the Spirit, ready for the next season of conquest. You may not be Jesus, but if you believe in Him you are a child of God. And that is frightening to hell because it means you have the possibility of making an eternal difference today.

Sometimes that conflict at work isn't just two personalities clashing; it's three. But if you pray, our Father will give you the answer to overcome it. Sometimes that pressure you feel at home isn't just the normal stuff of life; it's the influence of the Tempter seeking to steal your joy in Christ and make you do something that would be hurtful to others. But if you pray, our Father will show you how to turn that around for His glory. Sometimes the desire to have what belongs to someone else—house, car, promotion, spouse, etc.—is more than just lust; it's a strategy designed to destroy your destiny. But if you pray, our Father will release you from that false need and fulfill you with the real stuff of His Spirit.

Yesterday is gone and tomorrow may never come.

Today, if you hear His voice, do not harden your hearts (Hebrews 3:15).

Pray!

---

[1] Barnes' Notes, Albert Barnes, 1997 Biblesoft.
[2] Jerry Bridges, The Joy of Fearing God, (Waterbrook Press, 1997)
[3] Mychal F. Judge, Article from Sacramento Bee, February 2, 2002, "Personal Prayer Touches Many", Jennifer Garza
[4] Alexander MacLaren, Expositions of Holy Scripture, Hodder & Stoughton, New York, St. Mathew Chapter 1-8, p. 254
[5] Alexander MacLaren, Expositions of Holy Scripture, Hodder & Stoughton, New York, St. Mathew Chapter 1-8, p. 254.
[6] Joshua 24:15.
[7] John Ortberg , Toils, Dangers, and Snares: Resisting the Hidden Temptations of Ministry (Multnomah, 1994, p. 99-100).
[8] C.S. Lewis, Mere Christianity, HarperCollins Publishers, Inc., New York, NY 10022; p. 117.

To order additional copies of

OUR FATHER

Have your credit card ready and call:

1-877-421-READ (7323)

or please visit our web site at
www.pleasantword.com

Also available at: www.amazon.com

Printed in the United States
1471800002BA/1-39